LIFE STYLE DAILY
AFFIRMATIONS

LIFE STYLE DAILY AFFIRMATIONS

30 days of Motivational Readings to Build a
Positive Mindset

BERNARD DYSON

Introduction

Life Style Daily Affirmation book provides daily affirmations to help you get through life. This book will encourage you to find your passion, think about your life, create habits that will lead to you being a better person, and provide continuous empowerment to reach success. Over the different phases of my life, hard work, treating people right, and grinding day in and day out have been my focus. Over the years, I had to learn that being a good man was not good enough and that hard work did not always yield the type of success that I wanted. I had to learn to think through my next moves, identify what I really wanted in life, and figure out where I was currently in life before I could see where I wanted to go and accomplish. I had to learn that my asks to God had to be specific, by praying with a purpose and executing day in and day out. I had to get tired of my family not having what they deserved and going without at times. I had to get tired of me not doing enough to be successful and had to grind harder. A lot of days, I cried and did not know why life was dealing me bad hands. I had to fight for what I wanted, whether it was to get my business launched, get that job I wanted, build that home my wife and I wanted, and build a better life for my family and me. Once I realized that no one was coming to save me and God was the one I had to lean on, my vision got clearer. I could hear God's voice loud and clear, I upped my ask, doors started opening that before seemed impossible, and everything I lost was given back to me tenfold. Do not get it twisted, my faith was still assessed and still is, but I have learned how to cooperate with life, take the hits, and keep going. I had to learn that my struggles and pains are the testament that God allowed me to go through to author this book and share it with the world. So, I hope you enjoy yourself and find strength to keep going. I pray that everyone that reads this takes something back to their family to continue to spread love, build positive habits, finds empowerment to believe in themselves, and regains their imagination to believe that anything is possible with the right mindset. It takes 30 days to build a habit, and there are 30 days of daily affirmations to help you become a better person. Enjoy, take notes, take life seriously, and WIN! The choice is yours!

Day 1
BELIEVE IN YOURSELF WHEN NO ONE ELSE WILL

Believe in yourself when no one else does. In life, you must get tired of waiting on others to validate you and give yourself your own flowers for all that you have endeavored and accomplished. When people see the greatness inside of you, they should motivate and elevate your greatness through positive and honest feedback. If people are haters and make your life harder is up to you to be mentally and physically tough to still know who you are. You must be strong in the mist of jealousy, ignore the negative noise, realize the fake from the real, and still give your best when adversity strikes. Great people face challenges with a can-do attitude and believe that they will get through that moment. When you execute and make the choice to pursue your dreams, visions, and goals, the pressure and adversity starts. The reason is because you have made a choice to seek greatness and now the devil will start attacking you to see if you will easily give up. Your armor and shield will be your strong will, faith, and self-affirmation to believe in you. I have been the victim of intentional career sabotaging, and the ones doing it never thought I knew what they were doing it. I have been the victim of folks claiming to be supportive, until you surpass them in life, even though you never changed. As you encounter success, know your worth, create and build a confidence that no one can destroy and a confidence that is embedded in your character, like blood running through your veins. As you identify who you are, remain true to your authentic self and value yourself enough not to give time and effort to things and people that do not deserve it. Create or identify your true support system, and never let go of those individuals. Finally, always take care of you before you can take care of anyone else. Release the other people that always doubt you, the ones that always talk negative about you, and the ones that display fake love just to see how far you will take your success. Use the negative noise as empowerment and motivation to be great in all that you do to accomplish your dreams, visions, and goals.

Life is about facing challenges head on and not shying away from a fight. Fighting means fighting with yourself to stay disciplined, fighting to control your emotions, fighting to work in silence, fighting to know when to walk away from someone because they are a dream killer, fighting to take care of yourself mentally and physically, and fighting to never give up on your dreams, visions, and goals. You got this!

Day 2
EXECUTION

Do not just talk about it, be about it. Put your dreams, visions, and goals into the universe. Tell the world that you are coming and no one or nothing is going to stop you from being successful in life. If you want to be a millionaire, claim it. If you want to be wealthy, claim it. If there is something you desire in life, claim it. Sometimes, we spend too much time trying to make others believe in us, but that time and effort should be focused on making yourself believe in you. Be proud of who you are, go after your dreams no matter how long it takes to obtain them, hold yourself accountable, put in the work every single day, and execute with a purpose in all that you do. You get out of life what you pour into it. Life Style Motivation by Bernard Dyson Jr.

Day 3
TIME TO BE POSITIVELY CONSISTENT
TO CHANGE THE CULTURE

Be positively consistent in all your efforts and winning will always be a part of your character. Give the world a reason to talk about the remarkable things you do in life. Be consistent by being a great leader, by being a great listener, by being a great communicator, by being a great person, by being a notable example for yourself and others. Folks do not always praise you for doing something positive or good or great things but are always ready to talk when you do something bad. We must stop waiting for our fellow men or women to fail and motivate and elevate them. There are too many kids looked over because no one acknowledged their good behavior, too many employees that leave companies because no one said, "I see you or Thank you", there are too many relationships that failed because no one wanted to offer advice, and there are too many people that are too proud to acknowledge that their peer is a true champion. It is time to change the culture. Are you helping or destroying the culture? Life Style Motivation.

Day 4
LET GO OF THE PAST

You may forgive but you never forget, right? People may have intentionally hurt you or caused pain, but it is time to move on. It is time to use that pain to regain your strength, refocus, self-reflect, outshine, and prove to those that doubt you that they do not control your success. Living in the past causes you to neglect your tomorrow and even will cause you to hurt others or yourself. Living in the past will make you not see your own greatness, while trying to be something or someone you have outgrown. So, today, focus on living for today because you are great beyond measure. Know that your life is precious, and you must live to be happy with who you are and know that you have a lot more living and love to give. Know that you are already blessed. Now release the past, use the pain to keep going, and do not stop being great! If you live in the past, those that caused the pain will win if you do not hit the winning shot. Life Style Motivation by Bernard Dyson Jr

Day 5
REMOVE THE FEAR OF SUCCESS

A lot of the time, we are more fearful of success than we are of failure. In most instances, we fail more than we succeed and that causes us to expect failure. All it takes is for you to win one time, even after failing one hundred times. All that matters is that you never give/gave up. Success is a part of the unknown but worth the fight, failures, and worth seeing how it can mentally, emotionally, and physically improve your life. People will talk about you when you lose and they will talk about you when you win. Today, eliminate thinking about what folks will say, be motivated to succeed, do not give up no matter how many times you fail, stop procrastinating, and run after your dreams, visions, and goals. You are one step away from winning. Life Style Motivation by Bernard Dyson Jr.

Day 6
IF YOU WANT A BETTER LIFE, DO MORE

What are you not doing that you should be doing to live a better life and/or to be a better person? In life, we spend too much time focusing on why and how something happened, instead of focusing on giving max effort and giving our full self to whatever that task or job was. If you want more, you must be willing to give more and do more for your own self-edification and self-accountability. Therefore, when something does not go as planned, you do not have any regrets, but you learn from it, adjust, control your emotions, and keep grinding. It is not about how you start but how you finish. Make them remember you through your hard work. Life Style Motivation by Bernard Dyson Jr.

Day 7
PUSH THROUGH LIFE'S CHALLENGES
AND OBSTACLES

I was having a conversation with my 5-year-old son about school and what is challenging for him at school. Kids have the mindset that nothing is hard because they have the imagination to believe that anything is possible. My son told me nothing at school was hard. My motto for him is to never give up when life gets hard. He told me that when things get hard, you must have perseverance to push through life's challenges and obstacles.

Today, have perseverance to push through all life challenges and obstacles. If you do not give up, you will make it through it and a life lesson will be learned. Nothing in life can defeat you when you face it head on and stand your ground. So, you control your next move, remain disciplined and positive, do not give in to unhealthy stress, shock the world by believing in yourself, take the punches, but get back up and show the world that you will not be defeated or overlooked. It is your turn. Life Style Motivation by Bernard Dyson Jr

Day 8
YOU MUST BELIEVE

If you believe in it, your dream can come true. If you write it down, you then can see it and watch it come to fruition. Most folks believe that only young people can dream and have goals. Only older or seasoned folks have wisdom. Only people who have money can get nice things. You must have the right education to be successful. If you limit your ability by thinking like everyone else, you will never be successful or reach your goals. Dream big and go after it. Have faith that if you want something, God will make a way. If you put in the work, your hopes and dreams will become reality. See yourself at the top of the mountain, believe that you belong, and know that life is not over unless you give up on yourself. No matter what, you can have whatever you want in life.

There is not anything on this earth that you cannot do with the right mindset. So run after your dreams with a purpose. Do not let anyone make you feel like you are beneath them because all people were created equal. If you must grind harder, do it. If you must give more effort today than yesterday, do it. Stay on your path because the finish line is closer than you think. Stay

disciplined and stay motivated. Life Style Motivation by
Bernard Dyson Jr.

Day 9
EVERYONE CAN DREAM BIG

The ability to believe in the unknown and dream of the impossible is a gift. The ability to believe in others and encourage others to live life without regrets is called passion. The ability to be unselfish in your thoughts and want others to succeed is called caring. The ability to help others manifest their full potential through positive good will is called grace. Believing that you have a purpose and living in your purpose with kindness for the betterment and success of you, your family, and the life of others is called favor. Are you living or just existing? Are you making the world a better place or corrupting it with your own thoughts about others? Your inner thoughts will block your greatness and success if allowed. It's time to change our mindsets. Life Style Motivation by Bernard Dyson Jr.

Day 10
BE A PERSON OF VALUE

Be the type of person that people admire, not because you are perfect, but because you are honest, trustworthy, have a big heart, stand up for business, and encourage. Be the type of person that does not stand for foolishness and knows when, where, and how to stand up for what is right. Be the type of person that chooses to stand alone and fight for your future, even when you must walk alone. Be mentally tough and do not allow yourself to be fooled, because trouble does not always last. Be great, because being good is overrated. Life Style Motivation by Bernard Dyson Jr.

Day 11
DO NOT GIVE UP

If you are looking to give up today, do not because quitting is not part of your character. You can and will do whatever it is you are trying to accomplish. If you are stressed today, continue to work on the work, and do not let the work deter you. Continue to do all you can by prepping, brainstorming, being observant, and executing. If you cannot find a smile, please do it because smiling releases stress and allows you to think clearly. If you thought you would simply be good today, be great today because greatness is inside of you. So, dig deep today, take off the stress, and do not fail the test by giving in to negativity. Life Style Motivation by Bernard Dyson Jr

Day 12
HELP NOT HATE

The world is full of enough hate, haters, non-believers, folks that don't want to see others succeed whether you say it verbally or within your thoughts, backbiters, fake friends, and non-positive people that will destroy your confidence if allowed. Be someone that makes others smile, someone that encourages others, someone that gives without expecting something in return, someone that is willing to teach or extend your hand to help, someone that sees the good in people until they show you something different, and someone that gives off positive vibes. This does not mean that you run up to everyone but it does mean that you are authentic and kind. So, are you destroying another's confidence, being honest and encouraging from the heart or being a positive motivator? Life Style Motivation by Bernard Dyson Jr.

Day 13
KEEP LIFE SIMPLE AND DO NOT OVERTHINK IT

A lot of times we expect the road chosen to be rough and difficult but, in most cases, God makes the path smooth and durable. Meaning success is not easy but not as hard as we thought it would be. To live a full circle life, you must stay on the path even when the enemy jumps from all angles to pull you backwards or discourage you. A lot of the time, the enemy is us. If you want something in life, go get it, grind nonstop, have grit, be willing to fight to keep your mind and will power, and don't stop until you run over the finish line - which is the goal/ reason you stayed on the road in the first place. Keeping life simple is a fundamental part of life. Life Style Motivation by Bernard Dyson Jr.

Day 14
REGAIN YOUR CHILDLIKE IMAGINATION

Regain that inner child way of thinking, where you believed that anything and everything was possible. As a child, your imagination was without limits and your creativity was free flowing. Today, give yourself life once again and believe in yourself. Life sometimes forces us to think inside a box or only focus on where you are in life now and makes you think that your dreams, visions, and goals are no longer worth pursuing. It is time to live life and enjoy life for all that it has to offer. If you regain the right mindset, your body will follow, happiness will be revealed, and the passion for your reason to keep living will be replenished. You have more living to do. Life Style Motivation by Bernard Dyson Jr.

Day 15
STOP MAKING IRRATIONAL DECISIONS
BASED ON YOUR EMOTIONS

As leaders, fathers, mothers, and/or people in a position of power, we must base our decisions on facts or evidence not our feelings. One irrational decision can impact the life of another. Always get both sides of the story, always think about the big picture, and always be willing to stand by the decision you made whether wrong or right. As a leader, be willing to admit if you made a mistake, be willing to listen to your people, and always be transparent as much as possible. As a leader, making tough decisions is hard but necessary. So always know how to lead from the front and from the back.

Day 16
(INTERMISSION) - TIME TO RECHARGE

You have made it halfway through your journey to becoming a better person. Continue to implement what you have learned and read into your daily life. You may feel mentally drained because you are fighting to be different in an effective way but stay on the positive path. You are closer than you think and can and will get through this.

Recharging is another word for refueling. It is time to get tired of struggling, tired of not having what you want in life, tired of being treated disrespectfully, tired of not living a full life, tired of unhealthy stress, and/or tired of whatever has been holding you back in life. Meaning you must have been going through something that has caused you to get tired or need just a little bit more effort and energy to get through that situation. Think of it like exercising or driving a car. The more you push yourself, the more energy you exhaust which causes your energy level to run low. Now you need that second wind because you know how it feels to get tired. Now let's look at your life. In life you must get tired of being average, tired of struggling, and tired of not having what you want. It is time to give max effort and refuel with the necessities needed to reach your dreams, visions, and goals. Sometimes your momentum and energy are being put towards the wrong things or you are going in the wrong direction away from where God is trying to take you. So, you keep refueling with the wrong type of gas, using unleaded, when God has chosen you to use premium gas. In life, we must first set goals and write them down. For me, I ran from my calling of ministry away from God, and at the same time, God gave me the choice to do so. Do not get me wrong, I was still being a good father, husband, coworker, friend, son, brother, whatever but God wanted to elevate me to greatness. So, what did I do to recharge my life in the right direction and gain momentum? I wrote down everything I wanted in life. My wife and I wrote down the type of home we wanted to build, I wrote down the job I wanted, I wrote down the business plan I wanted. Then I started executing and talking to God and believing that my family and I deserved these things and started executing and allowing God to lead me. So, my faith increased, I became emotionally stable, I had a true purpose, my work ethic increased, and then the blessings started overflowing. Now that I have recharged, I have momentum to push through everything, even on days that I am humanly tired - this momentum. So, what now? Here comes adversity to try and distract you and make you quit but do not give in. Following God, now being a great man, and giving max effort my wife and I lost a child. So now I must check myself and determine if I need to keep using premium gas or go back to unleaded because I am in pain. No, I cannot because I have people depending on me to keep going. I am the glue. I had to check my mental status, go through grief, and continue to support my wife and family. So, in life, just know that it is not the adversity you go through that defines you, it is the way you manage the adversity to maintain your character to continue to be great.

Day 18
STOP BEING JUDGMENTAL

Challenge yourself to think differently by removing judgement from people that do not look like you. Challenge yourself to accept that life only has limits if you set them yourself. Challenge yourself to step outside of what our elders did and use that as motivation to embrace change by learning from the past. Challenge yourself to stand for something that will impact not only your life, but others as well. It is time to see the beauty of a person's heart and intelligence not their outward appearance, because that just might be the next leader, president, business CEO, billionaire, or the one you might need help from one day. It is time to be impactful. Life Style Motivation by Bernard Dyson Jr.

Day 19
YOU ARE A WINNER

Be a winner in all that you do. Be the type of winner that uses your time wisely to reach your greatness. Meaning, you may have sleepless nights or long days, but in the end the sacrifices will be worth it. If you grind hard now, the rest of your life will be easier and more abundant. Easy means more doors, more opportunities, more sources of income, more love, more faith, more celebrations, and more wins. Believe that you can win, execute, and do not let anything or no one stop you. The sky is the limit. Life Style Motivation by Bernard Dyson Jr.

Day 20
BE A WARRIOR

Warriors defend themselves and fight confidently to protect their kingdom. Your kingdom is you. You are a temple worth fighting for and your support system is worth fighting for. Be a warrior and do not stop fighting for you and all that you want in life, until you win. Losing is a part of winning if you get up each time you fall. Be the warrior that is unstoppable, that no one can defeat. Pain, depression, heartbreak, loss, words, another's pain, feeling sorry for yourself, or whatever will/should not stop you from fighting. Release the warrior in you. Life Style Motivation by Bernard Dyson Jr.

Day 21
BE GRATEFUL FOR THE LITTLE THINGS AS YOU PREPARE FOR GREATER BLESSINGS

Be grateful for the little things in life, as you press forward to reach greatness. It sucks to go through obstacles that cause us pain but those are the moments that define you as a true warrior. You just cannot give up in the mist of fighting through whatever it is mentally or physically that is bothering you. You must be strong, embrace the process, continue to grind every day, outline a game plan to get through it, and have faith that God will not fail you.

Be specific with your ask to God, no matter how far-fetched or unrealistic they may seem to man. You know exactly what you want and what you need. So, stop settling for less when there are no limits to the power of God. Continue to have faith, continue to grind even if you get tired, continue to execute even on days you do not know how to proceed, continue to be a great man or woman, and continue to watch God move. You can and will go farther with God, rather than trying to do it alone. Life Style Motivation by Bernard Dyson Jr.

Day 22

YOU ARE A DIAMOND

Are you worth fighting for? There may have been multiple moments of pain that have occurred in your life, but you must believe that you are still a diamond. Your life is precious. Your future does not have to be like your past. You made it despite the hard times. It is time to shed that layer of non-belief and step into the new you or should I say, reveal the improved you to the world. It is time to polish up the old you and be the diamond you were made to be. No more hiding the sparkle that glows within you. No more limitations on your worth because you are priceless. Shine bright today and go and be great because you are worth fighting for first. Now go accomplish your dreams, visions, and goals.

Day 23
SHARING KNOWLEDGE RESEMBLES POWER

When you help someone else succeed, you will indeed be rewarded for that effort. Caring about the well-being of others enough to want them to succeed just as much as you are called Power. Meaning providing opportunities when enemies run. Think of teaching like a kid learning math and/or sight words. When a kid teaches others, in that process they learn things about themselves and get better. As people, we must do the same to be a better person and help improve the lives of others. Self-actualization is the name of the game. When you enjoy what you do and do it out of kindness, money, favor, love, and blessings will overflow. Are you using your power in the right way? Or are you hindering your blessings and the blessings of others? What are you doing to help others? Life Style Motivation by Bernard Dyson Jr.

Day 24

RELEASE THE STRESS, ELEVATE YOUR LIFE, AND ALLOW GOD TO LEAD YOU

When you release all the burdens that are holding you back in life, you release God to do his work. Those burdens may be situations or circumstances that you have no control over or a situation you need a solution to. Once you release them to God and allow him to walk in front of you, no one or anything can block your greatness. Now that your mind is free of all the clutter, you can see where you need to go, who you need to reach out to, what door just opened, and when it is time to move or stand still. Know that you are a masterpiece that is valuable to you and priceless to the world. Stop allowing others to limit what you can or cannot do to have the lifestyle you want.

Release the stress of the world, regain your focus, and think about your next move in life. Your next move could change your life in a major way, only if you step out onto Faith Street. It is time to execute on the visions and dreams that keep you up at night. Stop holding back and stop procrastinating. You are one move away from success and winning. On your mark, get set,

GO! No one can stop or defeat you. The only limitations are the ones you set, as it is time to elevate. Life Style Motivation by Bernard Dyson Jr.

Day 25
STOP MAKING EXCUSES, STOP
WORRYING, AND STAY ON TRACK

You prayed and asked God for more, a better life, and to show you the path to take. Now that he has given it to you and granted your wishes, you have decided to procrastinate and doubt that you can do it. Today it is time to refocus and gain strength and momentum to keep going. Sometimes we must wait for great things to happen and then other times, great things come much sooner than expected. You must mentally and physically stay ready to continue running toward your dreams, visions, and goals. So, dig deep and regain your confidence, believe that you deserve everything you prayed for, and remain humble as the doors open. It is your turn, so claim it.

Get out of your own way and stop making life harder than it is. Sometimes we tell ourselves that something is going to be difficult in our minds and before you know it, you do not even try to pursue it. Greatness requires sacrifice and will be challenging at times but that does not mean that you cannot accomplish what you set your mind to do. If you keep making excuses, you will never get to the next level. It is time to find a way up the ladder and claim your place in society for the lifestyle you want. Life Style Motivation by Bernard Dyson Jr.

Day 26
EVERY ACTION HAS A REACTION

Every opportunity is an opportunity for learning, self-reflection, and development. Everything you do impacts the life of another through your communication, behavioral output - negative or positive, or simply through those that look up to you knowingly or unknowingly. Think before you speak, look before you reach, practice what you preach, and own up to your mistakes. Hold yourself accountable for your actions. You will not be perfect in all you do but strive to be in a positive light. If you change your life, you will change and impact the lives of others. If you only believe...

Everyone has an opportunity to be great if you only believe that anything is possible. Retrain your mind to remove self-doubt and be great. Being great means turning yourself into a fully well-rounded person that uses every obstacle to improve your-self and the others around you. Step into your destiny with boldness and a will to fight, no matter who or what tries to block your success. You either go through them or around them, proving that you will not be denied what is yours. Stop being scared and go be great. Life Style Motivation by Bernard Dyson Jr.

Day 27
THE ART OF SILENCE TO CONTROL
YOUR EMOTIONS

Silence does not always mean that a person is dumb, not paying attention, and/or neglecting the moment. Silence is a part of critical thinking and the first part of listening for better communication and understanding. Silence brings patience and along comes wisdom, which forces one to think before they react or say something negative that destroys everything you have built and worked for. Silence can mean that one is focused and on a path that others do not understand, but on a path to greatness - waiting to defeat the odds of all their haters with success. Silence can also mean fear or danger. Meaning quiet before the storm and as always, a storm leaves pain, disappointment, hurt, or a bad impression that will follow you for the rest of your life. Which side of silence are you on? Are you causing others to be silent due to negativity? Today, use your silence in the right way to promote positive impacts on your life and others. The choice to be great is up to you. Life Style Motivation by Bernard Dyson Jr.

Day 28
BE A CHAMPION OF YOUR LIFE

Life is about wins and losses because losses are what build character and elevate your discipline. If you have failed or struggled in the mist of adversity, you know how it feels to feel defeated, down, or lost to where you want to give up. On the other side, you have learned what not to do, how to get up, how to fight back, and where you do not want to go back to. Life is like a boxing ring. You can dance in it, you can run in it, you can lay down in it, or you can stand up and fight to have the life you want. If life knocks you down in the first round because you did not know how to defend yourself or what punch was coming, get back up and fight. Learn how to bob and weave, learn how to move to avoid hits, and learn what not to do from your previous mistakes. It is not how you start; it is how you finish. So, defeat the odds and prove the haters wrong. It is time to be a champion. Life Style Motivation by Bernard Dyson Jr.

———————————

Day 29
COMMITMENT AND ACCOUNTABILITY

———————————

Do you live and die by the commitments you make to yourself and others? Meaning don't just say things verbally just for the moment to only satisfy a question or to get someone off your back, when you know you need to do better... Always be a person of value and ensure that your actions align with your promises to your family, to yourself, to your job, to your clients, friends, and/or colleagues. No matter how high or low you are on the mountain, you will always need help. So, commit yourself to being accountable and taking life seriously. That promise that you made could be life or death for that person if you take it lightly. Be different in a positive way and allow your words and actions to be bonds of commitment. Life Style Motivation by Bernard Dyson Jr.

Day 30
PRACTICE SELF CARE AND STOP BEING LAZY

Self-care is super important before you can step into your next phase of life for the betterment of your life and/or before you can help others. Today make yourself a priority. Start enhancing your intelligence by reading positive affirmations, start grooming and getting your hair done, stop waiting until you must go somewhere to look nice, start dressing to impress yourself, start showering and brushing your teeth for good hygiene, put on some smell goods and dance in the beautiful aroma, and tell yourself that you are worth it. Sometimes we can get comfortable not being seen and allow laziness to set in, but it is time to do better. Start back loving you today and get your life back.

Put your energy into committing to being a better you. Meaning do not set goals if you do not want to discipline yourself to accomplish them and do not neglect the hard work it will take to get there. It is up to you to motivate yourself to reach greatness, but you must have the willpower to win. It is time to press play in your life and do not stop until the script reflects an image of which you are proud. Create the lifestyle you want starting today. Life Style Motivation by Bernard Dyson Jr.

Day 31
RUN AFTER YOUR DREAMS, VISIONS, AND GOALS

Use the good and bad times as motivation to create and maintain a better you. Everything that you go through in life should be stored and used as energy to help push you to greatness. So internally you already are what you want to be. You just need to start believing in yourself and getting rid of doubts. Once you believe, now you can release what is within you to be anything and everything you put your mind to. So dig deep. Release the beast inside of you and get what is yours. Life Style Motivation by Bernard Dyson Jr.

Adversity has ruined your life for far too long because you never felt like you had a way out or knew that you had a choice to fight back. Today, it is time to be a new you and allow the world to see the new you. As you wrap up reading this book of affirmations, use them frequently for the betterment of your lifestyle. You now have the tools to live a more fulfilling life mentally, physically, and spiritually. One key takeaway is to become spiritually grounded in your life. The power of prayer and having a spiritual relationship with God is needed in your life to defeat the evil that the devil throws at you. As adults, we sometimes are not strong enough to fight negativity and evil alone, and we need help to get through life situations. So, pray for protection, pray for a covenant over your life and your family's life, pray for a release of blessings, and pray for the good and bad times that you encounter in life. Have faith in the mist of adversity that you will make it through it if you commit to not being defeated. Sometimes you must humble yourself and ask for God's help and for him to intervene on your behalf. But always remember that if you glorify him on the good and bad days and do not just call on him in miin the mistrouble, he will never leave you and always will have your back. When doors open that you did not even ask for, that is favor from God.

Know that you are a winner and have a reason to live because your life is precious. Now it is time for you to execute to bring your dreams, visions, and goals into existence. Do not stop running after the life you want, but just know that you can do it and will be successful.

I am so proud of you because unbelievably, you have created a positive habit by reading these affirmations until the end. So, smile, spread love, believe in yourself, and continue to create the life style you want.

"Create the lifestyle you want by executing daily and maintaining a positive attitude!"
By Bernard Dyson Jr

www.ingramcontent.com/pod-product-compliance
Lightning Source LLC
Chambersburg PA
CBHW020654160726
47991CB00003B/1181